2021-2022

Two Year Monthly Planner and Calendar

I0384898

2021-2022 Two Year Monthly Planner and Calendar

First paperback edition December 2020

PERSONAL INFORMATION

NAME	
ADDRESS	
CITY	STATE
HOME	CELL
EMAIL	
COMPANY NAME	
ADDRESS	
CITY	STATE
PHONE	CELL
EMAIL	
DOCTOR	
DENTIST	
ALLERGIES	
BLOOD TYPE	
ESSENTIAL INFORMATION	
EMERGENCY	
NOTIFY & RELATIONSHIPS	
ADDRESS	
CITY	STATE
PHONE	CELL
EMAIL	

PERSONAL EMERGENCY CONTACT LIST

Local Contact	
Name:	
Address:	
Telephone:	

Nearest Relative	
Name:	
Address:	
Telephone:	

Family work & cell phone numbers	
1	
2	
3	
4	

Out-of-area contact	
Name:	
Address:	
Telephone:	

Children's school/Daycare provider	
School/Daycare:	
School/Daycare:	
School/Daycare:	
School/Daycare:	

CONTACTS

Name:	
Phone Number:	
Email:	
Address:	
Name:	
Phone Number:	
Email:	
Address:	
Name:	
Phone Number:	
Email:	
Address:	
Name:	
Phone Number:	
Email:	
Address:	
Name:	
Phone Number:	
Email:	
Address:	

CONTACTS

Name:	
Phone Number:	
Email:	
Address:	
Name:	
Phone Number:	
Email:	
Address:	
Name:	
Phone Number:	
Email:	
Address:	
Name:	
Phone Number:	
Email:	
Address:	
Name:	
Phone Number:	
Email:	
Address:	

CONTACTS

Name:	
Phone Number:	
Email:	
Address:	
Name:	
Phone Number:	
Email:	
Address:	
Name:	
Phone Number:	
Email:	
Address:	
Name:	
Phone Number:	
Email:	
Address:	
Name:	
Phone Number:	
Email:	
Address:	

CONTACTS

Name:	
Phone Number:	
Email:	
Address:	
Name:	
Phone Number:	
Email:	
Address:	
Name:	
Phone Number:	
Email:	
Address:	
Name:	
Phone Number:	
Email:	
Address:	
Name:	
Phone Number:	
Email:	
Address:	

CONTACTS

Name:	
Phone Number:	
Email:	
Address:	
Name:	
Phone Number:	
Email:	
Address:	
Name:	
Phone Number:	
Email:	
Address:	
Name:	
Phone Number:	
Email:	
Address:	
Name:	
Phone Number:	
Email:	
Address:	

CONTACTS

Name:	
Phone Number:	
Email:	
Address:	
Name:	
Phone Number:	
Email:	
Address:	
Name:	
Phone Number:	
Email:	
Address:	
Name:	
Phone Number:	
Email:	
Address:	
Name:	
Phone Number:	
Email:	
Address:	

CONTACTS

Name:	
Phone Number:	
Email:	
Address:	
Name:	
Phone Number:	
Email:	
Address:	
Name:	
Phone Number:	
Email:	
Address:	
Name:	
Phone Number:	
Email:	
Address:	
Name:	
Phone Number:	
Email:	
Address:	

CONTACTS

Name:	
Phone Number:	
Email:	
Address:	
Name:	
Phone Number:	
Email:	
Address:	
Name:	
Phone Number:	
Email:	
Address:	
Name:	
Phone Number:	
Email:	
Address:	
Name:	
Phone Number:	
Email:	
Address:	

CONTACTS

Name:	
Phone Number:	
Email:	
Address:	
Name:	
Phone Number:	
Email:	
Address:	
Name:	
Phone Number:	
Email:	
Address:	
Name:	
Phone Number:	
Email:	
Address:	
Name:	
Phone Number:	
Email:	
Address:	

2021 CALENDAR

JANUARY

Mon	Tue	Wed	Thu	Fri	Sat	Sun
				1	2	3
4	5	6	7	8	9	10
11	12	13	14	15	16	17
18	19	20	21	22	23	24
25	26	27	28	29	30	31

FEBRUARY

Mon	Tue	Wed	Thu	Fri	Sat	Sun
1	2	3	4	5	6	7
8	9	10	11	12	13	14
15	16	17	18	19	20	21
22	23	24	25	26	27	28

MARCH

Mon	Tue	Wed	Thu	Fri	Sat	Sun
1	2	3	4	5	6	7
8	9	10	11	12	13	14
15	16	17	18	19	20	21
22	23	24	25	26	27	28
29	30	31				

APRIL

Mon	Tue	Wed	Thu	Fri	Sat	Sun
			1	2	3	4
5	6	7	8	9	10	11
12	13	14	15	16	17	18
19	20	21	22	23	24	25
26	27	28	29	30		

MAY

Mon	Tue	Wed	Thu	Fri	Sat	Sun
					1	2
3	4	5	6	7	8	9
10	11	12	13	14	15	16
17	18	19	20	21	22	23
24 / 31	25	26	27	28	29	30

JUNE

Mon	Tue	Wed	Thu	Fri	Sat	Sun
	1	2	3	4	5	6
7	8	9	10	11	12	13
14	15	16	17	18	19	20
21	22	23	24	25	26	27
28	29	30				

JULY

Mon	Tue	Wed	Thu	Fri	Sat	Sun
			1	2	3	4
5	6	7	8	9	10	11
12	13	14	15	16	17	18
19	20	21	22	23	24	25
26	27	28	29	30	31	

AUGUST

Mon	Tue	Wed	Thu	Fri	Sat	Sun
						1
2	3	4	5	6	7	8
9	10	11	12	13	14	15
16	17	18	19	20	21	22
23 / 30	24 / 31	25	26	27	28	29

SEPTEMBER

Mon	Tue	Wed	Thu	Fri	Sat	Sun
		1	2	3	4	5
6	7	8	9	10	11	12
13	14	15	16	17	18	19
20	21	22	23	24	25	26
27	28	29	30			

OCTOBER

Mon	Tue	Wed	Thu	Fri	Sat	Sun
				1	2	3
4	5	6	7	8	9	10
11	12	13	14	15	16	17
18	19	20	21	22	23	24
25	26	27	28	29	30	31

NOVEMBER

Mon	Tue	Wed	Thu	Fri	Sat	Sun
1	2	3	4	5	6	7
8	9	10	11	12	13	14
15	16	17	18	19	20	21
22	23	24	25	26	27	28
29	30					

DECEMBER

Mon	Tue	Wed	Thu	Fri	Sat	Sun
		1	2	3	4	5
6	7	8	9	10	11	12
13	14	15	16	17	18	19
20	21	22	23	24	25	26
27	28	29	30	31		

GOALS AND DREAMS

YEAR AT A GLANCE

January	February	March
April	May	June

Notes

2021

July	August	September
October	November	December

Notes

JANUARY

Goals

S	M	T	W	T	F	S
					1	2
3	4	5	6	7	8	9
10	11	12	13	14	15	16
17	18	19	20	21	22	23
24	25	26	27	28	29	30
31						

Important dates

Birthdays

MONTHLY BUDGET

Initial Balance

Fixed Expenses

Date	Description	Amount

Other Expenses

Date	Description	Amount

Income

Date	Description	Amount

Total Income...

Total Fixed Expenses.......

Total Other Expenses.......

Net Balance....

JANUARY

SUNDAY	MONDAY	TUESDAY	WEDNESDAY
3	4	5	6
10	11	12	13
17	18	19	20
24	25	26	27
31			

2021

THURSDAY	FRIDAY	SATURDAY
	1	2
7	8	9
14	15	16
21	22	23
28	29	30

To-Do List:

- [ ]
- [ ]
- [ ]
- [ ]
- [ ]
- [ ]
- [ ]
- [ ]
- [ ]
- [ ]
- [ ]

Notes:

FEBRUARY

Goals

S	M	T	W	T	F	S
	1	2	3	4	5	6
7	8	9	10	11	12	13
14	15	16	17	18	19	20
21	22	23	24	25	26	27
28						

Important dates

Birthdays

MONTHLY BUDGET

Initial Balance

Fixed Expenses

Date	Description	Amount

Other Expenses

Date	Description	Amount

Income

Date	Description	Amount

Total Income...

Total Fixed Expenses.......

Total Other Expenses.......

Net Balance....

FEBRUARY

SUNDAY	MONDAY	TUESDAY	WEDNESDAY
	1	2	3
7	8	9	10
14	15	16	17
21	22	23	24
28			

2021

THURSDAY	FRIDAY	SATURDAY
4	5	6
11	12	13
18	19	20
25	26	27

To-Do List:

- [ ]
- [ ]
- [ ]
- [ ]
- [ ]
- [ ]
- [ ]
- [ ]
- [ ]
- [ ]
- [ ]

Notes:

MARCH

Goals

S	M	T	W	T	F	S
	1	2	3	4	5	6
7	8	9	10	11	12	13
14	15	16	17	18	19	20
21	22	23	24	25	26	27
28	29	30	31			

Important dates

Birthdays

MONTHLY BUDGET

Initial Balance

Fixed Expenses

Date	Description	Amount

Other Expenses

Date	Description	Amount

Income

Date	Description	Amount

Total Income...

Total Fixed Expenses.......

Total Other Expenses.......

Net Balance....

MARCH

SUNDAY	MONDAY	TUESDAY	WEDNESDAY
	1	2	3
7	8	9	10
14	15	16	17
21	22	23	24
28	29	30	31

2021

THURSDAY	FRIDAY	SATURDAY
4	5	6
11	12	13
18	19	20
25	26	27

To-Do List:

- [ ]
- [ ]
- [ ]
- [ ]
- [ ]
- [ ]
- [ ]
- [ ]
- [ ]
- [ ]
- [ ]

Notes:

APRIL

Goals

S	M	T	W	T	F	S
				1	2	3
4	5	6	7	8	9	10
11	12	13	14	15	16	17
18	19	20	21	22	23	24
25	26	27	28	29	30	

Important dates

Birthdays

MONTHLY BUDGET

Initial Balance

Fixed Expenses

Date	Description	Amount

Other Expenses

Date	Description	Amount

Income

Date	Description	Amount

Total Income...

Total Fixed Expenses.......

Total Other Expenses.......

Net Balance....

APRIL

SUNDAY	MONDAY	TUESDAY	WEDNESDAY
4	5	6	7
11	12	13	14
18	19	20	21
25	26	27	28

2021

THURSDAY	FRIDAY	SATURDAY
1	2	3
8	9	10
15	16	17
22	23	24
29	30	

To-Do List:

- [ ]
- [ ]
- [ ]
- [ ]
- [ ]
- [ ]
- [ ]
- [ ]
- [ ]
- [ ]
- [ ]

Notes:

MAY

Goals

S	M	T	W	T	F	S
						1
2	3	4	5	6	7	8
9	10	11	12	13	14	15
16	17	18	19	20	21	22
23	24	25	26	27	28	29
30	31					

Important dates

Birthdays

MONTHLY BUDGET

Initial Balance

Fixed Expenses

Date	Description	Amount

Other Expenses

Date	Description	Amount

Income

Date	Description	Amount

Total Income...

Total Fixed Expenses.......

Total Other Expenses.......

Net Balance....

MAY

SUNDAY	MONDAY	TUESDAY	WEDNESDAY
2	3	4	5
9	10	11	12
16	17	18	19
23	24	25	26
30	31		

2021

THURSDAY	FRIDAY	SATURDAY
		1
6	7	8
13	14	15
20	21	22
27	28	29

To-Do List:

- [ ]
- [ ]
- [ ]
- [ ]
- [ ]
- [ ]
- [ ]
- [ ]
- [ ]
- [ ]
- [ ]

Notes:

JUNE

Goals

S	M	T	W	T	F	S
		1	2	3	4	5
6	7	8	9	10	11	12
13	14	15	16	17	18	19
20	21	22	23	24	25	26
27	28	29	30			

Important dates

Birthdays

MONTHLY BUDGET

Initial Balance

Fixed Expenses

Date	Description	Amount

Other Expenses

Date	Description	Amount

Income

Date	Description	Amount

Total Income...

Total Fixed Expenses.......

Total Other Expenses.......

Net Balance....

JUNE

SUNDAY	MONDAY	TUESDAY	WEDNESDAY
		1	2
6	7	8	9
13	14	15	16
20	21	22	23
27	28	29	30

2021

THURSDAY	FRIDAY	SATURDAY
3	4	5
10	11	12
17	18	19
24	25	26

To-Do List:

- [ ]
- [ ]
- [ ]
- [ ]
- [ ]
- [ ]
- [ ]
- [ ]
- [ ]
- [ ]
- [ ]

Notes:

JULY

Goals

S	M	T	W	T	F	S
				1	2	3
4	5	6	7	8	9	10
11	12	13	14	15	16	17
18	19	20	21	22	23	24
25	26	27	28	29	30	31

Important dates

Birthdays

MONTHLY BUDGET

Initial Balance

Fixed Expenses

Date	Description	Amount

Other Expenses

Date	Description	Amount

Income

Date	Description	Amount

Total Income...

Total Fixed Expenses.......

Total Other Expenses.......

Net Balance....

JULY

SUNDAY	MONDAY	TUESDAY	WEDNESDAY
4	5	6	7
11	12	13	14
18	19	20	21
25	26	27	28

2021

THURSDAY	FRIDAY	SATURDAY
1	2	3
8	9	10
15	16	17
22	23	24
29	30	31

To-Do List:

- [ ]
- [ ]
- [ ]
- [ ]
- [ ]
- [ ]
- [ ]
- [ ]
- [ ]
- [ ]
- [ ]

Notes:

AUGUST

Goals

S	M	T	W	T	F	S
1	2	3	4	5	6	7
8	9	10	11	12	13	14
15	16	17	18	19	20	21
22	23	24	25	26	27	28
29	30	31				

Important dates

Birthdays

MONTHLY BUDGET

Initial Balance

Fixed Expenses

Date	Description	Amount

Other Expenses

Date	Description	Amount

Income

Date	Description	Amount

Total Income...

Total Fixed Expenses.......

Total Other Expenses.......

Net Balance....

AUGUST

SUNDAY	MONDAY	TUESDAY	WEDNESDAY
1	2	3	4
8	9	10	11
15	16	17	18
22	23	24	25
29	30	31	

2021

THURSDAY	FRIDAY	SATURDAY
5	6	7
12	13	14
19	20	21
26	27	28

To-Do List:

- [ ]
- [ ]
- [ ]
- [ ]
- [ ]
- [ ]
- [ ]
- [ ]
- [ ]
- [ ]
- [ ]

Notes:

SEPTEMBER

Goals

S	M	T	W	T	F	S
			1	2	3	4
5	6	7	8	9	10	11
12	13	14	15	16	17	18
19	20	21	22	23	24	25
26	27	28	29	30		

Important dates

Birthdays

MONTHLY BUDGET

Initial Balance

Fixed Expenses

Date	Description	Amount

Other Expenses

Date	Description	Amount

Income

Date	Description	Amount

Total Income...

Total Fixed Expenses.......

Total Other Expenses.......

Net Balance....

SEPTEMBER

SUNDAY	MONDAY	TUESDAY	WEDNESDAY
			1
5	6	7	8
12	13	14	15
19	20	21	22
26	27	28	29

2021

THURSDAY	FRIDAY	SATURDAY
2	3	4
9	10	11
16	17	18
23	24	25
30		

To-Do List:

- [ ]
- [ ]
- [ ]
- [ ]
- [ ]
- [ ]
- [ ]
- [ ]
- [ ]
- [ ]
- [ ]

Notes:

OCTOBER

Goals

S	M	T	W	T	F	S
					1	2
3	4	5	6	7	8	9
10	11	12	13	14	15	16
17	18	19	20	21	22	23
24	25	26	27	28	29	30
31						

Important dates

Birthdays

MONTHLY BUDGET

Initial Balance

Fixed Expenses

Date	Description	Amount

Other Expenses

Date	Description	Amount

Income

Date	Description	Amount

Total Income...

Total Fixed Expenses.......

Total Other Expenses.......

Net Balance....

OCTOBER

SUNDAY	MONDAY	TUESDAY	WEDNESDAY
3	4	5	6
10	11	12	13
17	18	19	20
24	25	26	27
31			

2021

THURSDAY	FRIDAY	SATURDAY
	1	2
7	8	9
14	15	16
21	22	23
28	29	30

To-Do List:

- [ ]
- [ ]
- [ ]
- [ ]
- [ ]
- [ ]
- [ ]
- [ ]
- [ ]
- [ ]
- [ ]

Notes:

NOVEMBER

Goals

S	M	T	W	T	F	S
	1	2	3	4	5	6
7	8	9	10	11	12	13
14	15	16	17	18	19	20
21	22	23	24	25	26	27
28	29	30				

Important dates

Birthdays

MONTHLY BUDGET

Initial Balance

Fixed Expenses

Date	Description	Amount

Other Expenses

Date	Description	Amount

Income

Date	Description	Amount

Total Income...

Total Fixed Expenses.......

Total Other Expenses.......

Net Balance....

NOVEMBER

SUNDAY	MONDAY	TUESDAY	WEDNESDAY
	1	2	3
7	8	9	10
14	15	16	17
21	22	23	24
28	29	30	

2021

THURSDAY	FRIDAY	SATURDAY
4	5	6
11	12	13
18	19	20
25	26	27

To-Do List:

- [ ]
- [ ]
- [ ]
- [ ]
- [ ]
- [ ]
- [ ]
- [ ]
- [ ]
- [ ]
- [ ]

Notes:

DECEMBER

Goals

S	M	T	W	T	F	S
			1	2	3	4
5	6	7	8	9	10	11
12	13	14	15	16	17	18
19	20	21	22	23	24	25
26	27	28	29	30	31	

Important dates

Birthdays

MONTHLY BUDGET

Initial Balance

Fixed Expenses

Date	Description	Amount

Other Expenses

Date	Description	Amount

Income

Date	Description	Amount

Total Income...

Total Fixed Expenses.......

Total Other Expenses.......

Net Balance....

DECEMBER

SUNDAY	MONDAY	TUESDAY	WEDNESDAY
			1
5	6	7	8
12	13	14	15
19	20	21	22
26	27	28	29

2021

THURSDAY	FRIDAY	SATURDAY
2	3	4
9	10	11
16	17	18
23	24	25
30	31	

To-Do List:

- [ ]
- [ ]
- [ ]
- [ ]
- [ ]
- [ ]
- [ ]
- [ ]
- [ ]
- [ ]
- [ ]

Notes:

2022
CALENDAR

JANUARY

Mon	Tue	Wed	Thu	Fri	Sat	Sun
					1	2
3	4	5	6	7	8	9
10	11	12	13	14	15	16
17	18	19	20	21	22	23
24 31	25	26	27	28	29	30

FEBRUARY

Mon	Tue	Wed	Thu	Fri	Sat	Sun
	1	2	3	4	5	6
7	8	9	10	11	12	13
14	15	16	17	18	19	20
21	22	23	24	25	26	27
28						

MARCH

Mon	Tue	Wed	Thu	Fri	Sat	Sun
	1	2	3	4	5	6
7	8	9	10	11	12	13
14	15	16	17	18	19	20
21	22	23	24	25	26	27
28	29	30	31			

APRIL

Mon	Tue	Wed	Thu	Fri	Sat	Sun
				1	2	3
4	5	6	7	8	9	10
11	12	13	14	15	16	17
18	19	20	21	22	23	24
25	26	27	28	29	30	

MAY

Mon	Tue	Wed	Thu	Fri	Sat	Sun
						1
2	3	4	5	6	7	8
9	10	11	12	13	14	15
16	17	18	19	20	21	22
23 30	24 31	25	26	27	28	29

JUNE

Mon	Tue	Wed	Thu	Fri	Sat	Sun
		1	2	3	4	5
6	7	8	9	10	11	12
13	14	15	16	17	18	19
20	21	22	23	24	25	26
27	28	29	30			

JULY

Mon	Tue	Wed	Thu	Fri	Sat	Sun
				1	2	3
4	5	6	7	8	9	10
11	12	13	14	15	16	17
18	19	20	21	22	23	24
25	26	27	28	29	30	31

AUGUST

Mon	Tue	Wed	Thu	Fri	Sat	Sun
1	2	3	4	5	6	7
8	9	10	11	12	13	14
15	16	17	18	19	20	21
22	23	24	25	26	27	28
29	30	31				

SEPTEMBER

Mon	Tue	Wed	Thu	Fri	Sat	Sun
			1	2	3	4
5	6	7	8	9	10	11
12	13	14	15	16	17	18
19	20	21	22	23	24	25
26	27	28	29	30		

OCTOBER

Mon	Tue	Wed	Thu	Fri	Sat	Sun
					1	2
3	4	5	6	7	8	9
10	11	12	13	14	15	16
17	18	19	20	21	22	23
24 31	25	26	27	28	29	30

NOVEMBER

Mon	Tue	Wed	Thu	Fri	Sat	Sun
	1	2	3	4	5	6
7	8	9	10	11	12	13
14	15	16	17	18	19	20
21	22	23	24	25	26	27
28	29	30				

DECEMBER

Mon	Tue	Wed	Thu	Fri	Sat	Sun
			1	2	3	4
5	6	7	8	9	10	11
12	13	14	15	16	17	18
19	20	21	22	23	24	25
26	27	28	29	30	31	

GOALS AND DREAMS

YEAR AT A GLANCE

January	February	March
April	May	June

Notes

2022

July	August	September
October	November	December

Notes

JANUARY

Goals

S	M	T	W	T	F	S
						1
2	3	4	5	6	7	8
9	10	11	12	13	14	15
16	17	18	19	20	21	22
23	24	25	26	27	28	29
30	31					

Important dates

Birthdays

MONTHLY BUDGET

Initial Balance

Fixed Expenses

Date	Description	Amount

Other Expenses

Date	Description	Amount

Income

Date	Description	Amount

Total Income...

Total Fixed Expenses.......

Total Other Expenses.......

Net Balance....

JANUARY

SUNDAY	MONDAY	TUESDAY	WEDNESDAY
2	3	4	5
9	10	11	12
16	17	18	19
23	24	25	26
30	31		

2022

THURSDAY	FRIDAY	SATURDAY
		1
6	7	8
13	14	15
20	21	22
27	28	29

To-Do List:

- [ ]
- [ ]
- [ ]
- [ ]
- [ ]
- [ ]
- [ ]
- [ ]
- [ ]
- [ ]
- [ ]

Notes:

FEBRUARY

Goals

S	M	T	W	T	F	S
		1	2	3	4	5
6	7	8	9	10	11	12
13	14	15	16	17	18	19
20	21	22	23	24	25	26
27	28					

Important dates

Birthdays

MONTHLY BUDGET

Initial Balance

Fixed Expenses

Date	Description	Amount

Other Expenses

Date	Description	Amount

Income

Date	Description	Amount

Total Income...

Total Fixed Expenses.......

Total Other Expenses.......

Net Balance....

FEBRUARY

SUNDAY	MONDAY	TUESDAY	WEDNESDAY
		1	2
6	7	8	9
13	14	15	16
20	21	22	23
27	28		

2022

THURSDAY	FRIDAY	SATURDAY
3	4	5
10	11	12
17	18	19
24	25	26

To-Do List:

- [ ]
- [ ]
- [ ]
- [ ]
- [ ]
- [ ]
- [ ]
- [ ]
- [ ]
- [ ]
- [ ]

Notes:

MARCH

Goals

S	M	T	W	T	F	S
		1	2	3	4	5
6	7	8	9	10	11	12
13	14	15	16	17	18	19
20	21	22	23	24	25	26
27	28	29	30	31		

Important dates

Birthdays

MONTHLY BUDGET

Initial Balance	

Fixed Expenses

Date	Description	Amount

Other Expenses

Date	Description	Amount

Income

Date	Description	Amount

Total Income...	
Total Fixed Expenses.......	
Total Other Expenses.......	
Net Balance....	

MARCH

SUNDAY	MONDAY	TUESDAY	WEDNESDAY
		1	2
6	7	8	9
13	14	15	16
20	21	22	23
27	28	29	30

2022

THURSDAY	FRIDAY	SATURDAY
3	4	5
10	11	12
17	18	19
24	25	26
31		

To-Do List:

- [ ]
- [ ]
- [ ]
- [ ]
- [ ]
- [ ]
- [ ]
- [ ]
- [ ]
- [ ]
- [ ]

Notes:

APRIL

Goals

S	M	T	W	T	F	S
					1	2
3	4	5	6	7	8	9
10	11	12	13	14	15	16
17	18	19	20	21	22	23
24	25	26	27	28	29	30

Important dates

Birthdays

MONTHLY BUDGET

Initial Balance

Fixed Expenses

Date	Description	Amount

Other Expenses

Date	Description	Amount

Income

Date	Description	Amount

Total Income...

Total Fixed Expenses.......

Total Other Expenses.......

Net Balance....

APRIL

SUNDAY	MONDAY	TUESDAY	WEDNESDAY
3	4	5	6
10	11	12	13
17	18	19	20
24	25	26	27

2022

THURSDAY	FRIDAY	SATURDAY
	1	2
7	8	9
14	15	16
21	22	23
28	29	30

To-Do List:

- [ ]
- [ ]
- [ ]
- [ ]
- [ ]
- [ ]
- [ ]
- [ ]
- [ ]
- [ ]
- [ ]

Notes:

MAY

Goals

S	M	T	W	T	F	S
1	2	3	4	5	6	7
8	9	10	11	12	13	14
15	16	17	18	19	20	21
22	23	24	25	26	27	28
29	30	31				

Important dates

Birthdays

MONTHLY BUDGET

Initial Balance

Fixed Expenses

Date	Description	Amount

Other Expenses

Date	Description	Amount

Income

Date	Description	Amount

Total Income...

Total Fixed Expenses.......

Total Other Expenses.......

Net Balance....

MAY

SUNDAY	MONDAY	TUESDAY	WEDNESDAY
1	2	3	4
8	9	10	11
15	16	17	18
22	23	24	25
29	30	31	

2022

THURSDAY	FRIDAY	SATURDAY
5	6	7
12	13	14
19	20	21
26	27	28

To-Do List:

- [ ]
- [ ]
- [ ]
- [ ]
- [ ]
- [ ]
- [ ]
- [ ]
- [ ]
- [ ]
- [ ]

Notes:

JUNE

Goals

S	M	T	W	T	F	S
			1	2	3	4
5	6	7	8	9	10	11
12	13	14	15	16	17	18
19	20	21	22	23	24	25
26	27	28	29	30		

Important dates

Birthdays

MONTHLY BUDGET

Initial Balance

Fixed Expenses

Date	Description	Amount

Other Expenses

Date	Description	Amount

Income

Date	Description	Amount

Total Income...

Total Fixed Expenses.......

Total Other Expenses.......

Net Balance....

JUNE

SUNDAY	MONDAY	TUESDAY	WEDNESDAY
			1
5	6	7	8
12	13	14	15
19	20	21	22
26	27	28	29

2022

THURSDAY	FRIDAY	SATURDAY
2	3	4
9	10	11
16	17	18
23	24	25
30		

To-Do List:

- [ ]
- [ ]
- [ ]
- [ ]
- [ ]
- [ ]
- [ ]
- [ ]
- [ ]
- [ ]
- [ ]

Notes:

JULY

Goals

S	M	T	W	T	F	S
					1	2
3	4	5	6	7	8	9
10	11	12	13	14	15	16
17	18	19	20	21	22	23
24	25	26	27	28	29	30
31						

Important dates

Birthdays

MONTHLY BUDGET

Initial Balance

Fixed Expenses

Date	Description	Amount

Other Expenses

Date	Description	Amount

Income

Date	Description	Amount

Total Income...

Total Fixed Expenses.......

Total Other Expenses.......

Net Balance....

JULY

SUNDAY	MONDAY	TUESDAY	WEDNESDAY
4	5	6	7
11	12	13	14
18	19	20	21
25	26	27	28

2022

THURSDAY	FRIDAY	SATURDAY
	1	2
7	8	9
14	15	16
21	22	23
28	29	30

To-Do List:

- [ ]
- [ ]
- [ ]
- [ ]
- [ ]
- [ ]
- [ ]
- [ ]
- [ ]
- [ ]
- [ ]

Notes:

AUGUST

Goals

S	M	T	W	T	F	S
	1	2	3	4	5	6
7	8	9	10	11	12	13
14	15	16	17	18	19	20
21	22	23	24	25	26	27
28	29	30	31			

Important dates

Birthdays

MONTHLY BUDGET

Initial Balance	

Fixed Expenses

Date	Description	Amount

Other Expenses

Date	Description	Amount

Income

Date	Description	Amount

Total Income...	
Total Fixed Expenses.......	
Total Other Expenses.......	
Net Balance....	

AUGUST

SUNDAY	MONDAY	TUESDAY	WEDNESDAY
	1	2	3
7	8	9	10
14	15	16	17
21	22	23	24
28	29	30	31

2022

THURSDAY	FRIDAY	SATURDAY
4	5	6
11	12	13
18	19	20
25	26	27

To-Do List:

- [ ]
- [ ]
- [ ]
- [ ]
- [ ]
- [ ]
- [ ]
- [ ]
- [ ]
- [ ]
- [ ]

Notes:

SEPTEMBER

Goals

S	M	T	W	T	F	S
				1	2	3
4	5	6	7	8	9	10
11	12	13	14	15	16	17
18	19	20	21	22	23	24
25	26	27	28	29	30	

Important dates

Birthdays

MONTHLY BUDGET

Initial Balance

Fixed Expenses

Date	Description	Amount

Other Expenses

Date	Description	Amount

Income

Date	Description	Amount

Total Income...

Total Fixed Expenses.......

Total Other Expenses.......

Net Balance....

SEPTEMBER

SUNDAY	MONDAY	TUESDAY	WEDNESDAY
4	5	6	7
11	12	13	14
18	19	20	21
25	26	27	28

2022

THURSDAY	FRIDAY	SATURDAY
1	2	3
8	9	10
15	16	17
22	23	24
29	30	

To-Do List:

- [ ]
- [ ]
- [ ]
- [ ]
- [ ]
- [ ]
- [ ]
- [ ]
- [ ]
- [ ]
- [ ]

Notes:

OCTOBER

Goals

S	M	T	W	T	F	S
						1
2	3	4	5	6	7	8
9	10	11	12	13	14	15
16	17	18	19	20	21	22
23	24	25	26	27	28	29
30	31					

Important dates

Birthdays

MONTHLY BUDGET

Initial Balance

Fixed Expenses

Date	Description	Amount

Other Expenses

Date	Description	Amount

Income

Date	Description	Amount

Total Income...

Total Fixed Expenses.......

Total Other Expenses.......

Net Balance....

OCTOBER

SUNDAY	MONDAY	TUESDAY	WEDNESDAY
2	3	4	5
9	10	11	12
16	17	18	19
23	24	25	26
30	31		

2022

THURSDAY	FRIDAY	SATURDAY
		1
6	7	8
13	14	15
20	21	22
27	28	29

To-Do List:

- [ ]
- [ ]
- [ ]
- [ ]
- [ ]
- [ ]
- [ ]
- [ ]
- [ ]
- [ ]
- [ ]

Notes:

NOVEMBER

Goals

S	M	T	W	T	F	S
		1	2	3	4	5
6	7	8	9	10	11	12
13	14	15	16	17	18	19
20	21	22	23	24	25	26
27	28	29	30			

Important dates

Birthdays

MONTHLY BUDGET

Initial Balance

Fixed Expenses

Date	Description	Amount

Other Expenses

Date	Description	Amount

Income

Date	Description	Amount

Total Income...

Total Fixed Expenses.......

Total Other Expenses.......

Net Balance....

NOVEMBER

SUNDAY	MONDAY	TUESDAY	WEDNESDAY
		1	2
6	7	8	9
13	14	15	16
20	21	22	23
27	28	29	30

2022

THURSDAY	FRIDAY	SATURDAY
3	4	5
10	11	12
17	18	19
24	25	26

To-Do List:

- [ ]
- [ ]
- [ ]
- [ ]
- [ ]
- [ ]
- [ ]
- [ ]
- [ ]
- [ ]
- [ ]

Notes:

DECEMBER

Goals

S	M	T	W	T	F	S
				1	2	3
4	5	6	7	8	9	10
11	12	13	14	15	16	17
18	19	20	21	22	23	24
25	26	27	28	29	30	31

Important dates

Birthdays

MONTHLY BUDGET

Initial Balance

Fixed Expenses

Date	Description	Amount

Other Expenses

Date	Description	Amount

Income

Date	Description	Amount

Total Income...

Total Fixed Expenses.......

Total Other Expenses.......

Net Balance....

DECEMBER

SUNDAY	MONDAY	TUESDAY	WEDNESDAY
4	5	6	7
11	12	13	14
18	19	20	21
25	26	27	28

2022

THURSDAY	FRIDAY	SATURDAY
1	2	3
8	9	10
15	16	17
22	23	24
29	30	31

To-Do List:

- [ ]
- [ ]
- [ ]
- [ ]
- [ ]
- [ ]
- [ ]
- [ ]
- [ ]
- [ ]
- [ ]

Notes:

MOVIES & TV SHOW LIST

Movies and TV Shows	Seen	Rating
	○	☆☆☆☆☆
	○	☆☆☆☆☆
	○	☆☆☆☆☆
	○	☆☆☆☆☆
	○	☆☆☆☆☆
	○	☆☆☆☆☆
	○	☆☆☆☆☆
	○	☆☆☆☆☆
	○	☆☆☆☆☆
	○	☆☆☆☆☆
	○	☆☆☆☆☆
	○	☆☆☆☆☆
	○	☆☆☆☆☆
	○	☆☆☆☆☆
	○	☆☆☆☆☆
	○	☆☆☆☆☆
	○	☆☆☆☆☆
	○	☆☆☆☆☆
	○	☆☆☆☆☆
	○	☆☆☆☆☆
	○	☆☆☆☆☆
	○	☆☆☆☆☆
	○	☆☆☆☆☆
	○	☆☆☆☆☆
	○	☆☆☆☆☆
	○	☆☆☆☆☆
	○	☆☆☆☆☆
	○	☆☆☆☆☆
	○	☆☆☆☆☆

BOOKS

Title	Author	Rating
		☆☆☆☆☆
		☆☆☆☆☆
		☆☆☆☆☆
		☆☆☆☆☆
		☆☆☆☆☆
		☆☆☆☆☆
		☆☆☆☆☆
		☆☆☆☆☆
		☆☆☆☆☆
		☆☆☆☆☆
		☆☆☆☆☆
		☆☆☆☆☆
		☆☆☆☆☆
		☆☆☆☆☆
		☆☆☆☆☆
		☆☆☆☆☆
		☆☆☆☆☆
		☆☆☆☆☆
		☆☆☆☆☆
		☆☆☆☆☆
		☆☆☆☆☆
		☆☆☆☆☆
		☆☆☆☆☆
		☆☆☆☆☆
		☆☆☆☆☆
		☆☆☆☆☆
		☆☆☆☆☆
		☆☆☆☆☆
		☆☆☆☆☆

WEBSITES & PASSWORDS

Website	Username	Password

WEBSITES & PASSWORDS

Website	Username	Password

NOTES

We thank you for choosing us.
We would really appreciate if you leave us an honest review.
Until next time!

www.ingramcontent.com/pod-product-compliance
Lightning Source LLC
Chambersburg PA
CBHW081507080526
44589CB00017B/2686
* 9 7 8 1 8 0 1 3 2 8 3 3 3 *